TECHNOLOGY IN ACTION

SPORTS TECHNOLOGY

Neil Duncanson

The Bookwright Press
New York · 1992

Titles in this series

First published in the
United States in 1992 by
The Bookwright Press
387 Park Avenue South
New York, NY 10016

First published in 1991 by
Wayland (Publishers) Ltd
61 Western Road, Hove
East Sussex BN3 1JD, England

Library of Congress Cataloging-in-Publication Data
Duncanson, Neil.
    Sports technology / by Neil Duncanson.
       p.   cm.—(Technology in action)
    Includes index.
    Summary: Discusses the application of practical
and mechanical sciences to sports in areas such as
equipment, sports arenas, television coverage, and
performance-enhancing drugs.
    ISBN 0-531-18401-3
    1. Sports—Technological innovations—Juvenile
literature. [1. Sports—Technological innovations.]
I. Title. II. Series.
GV745.D86 1992
688.7—dc20
                                        91-17570
                                           CIP
                                           AC

Cover   Skiers have benefited from plastic and
synthetic materials, which have made skis lighter
and easier to maneuver.

Typeset by Direct Image Photosetting Limited,
Sussex, England
Printed in Italy by G. Canale & C.S.p.A., Turin

Contents

Above Technological advances in motorsports have increased speeds *and* safety. Some of today's powerboats are capable of speeds in excess of 136 mph (220 kph).

The popularity of sport has never been greater than it is today, and the signs are that its power and influence will increase into the next century.

The twentieth century has seen many changes in the way sports are played and the numbers of people who watch them. Television has turned many sports into giant businesses able to rival any multinational company.

Sports were once a weekend pastime that did not warrant technological interest. Today sports have the financial power and marketing appeal to demand and receive all that modern technology can offer. The companies who can supply this modern technology benefit by using sports coverage as a display window for their products.

Athletes, both men and women, now compete for massive prizes and demand the best of everything, from training programs, equipment and sportswear, to timing equipment and the best surfaces on which to perform. For their part, the paying public, with a wide variety of leisure interests from which to choose, also want the best. They want the best stadiums and the best television coverage so that they can watch their favorite sports played at the highest level.

The application of practical and mechanical sciences to sports has intensified as the twentieth century has progressed and will continue to raise standards in sports for those who enjoy taking part in sports and those who enjoy watching.

A floodlit international cricket match at Australia's Sydney Cricket Ground. Spectators want the best stadiums so that they can watch their favorite sports played at the highest level.

Sports arenas were built by many early civilizations. For example, the Romans built the first indoor stadium, the Colosseum, in Rome, between about AD 72 and AD 80. The remains of the giant oval structure, where ancient games and gladiatorial combat took place, can still be seen today. The Romans were well ahead of their time. In nineteenth-century Britain special indoor facilities for sports finnally began to appear. London's Royal Albert Hall, which was opened in 1871, was built to hold events such as concerts and sports tournaments, and the domed building is still used today for all kinds of sports, including tennis, boxing and basketball.

The site of Madison Square Garden, in New York, one of the world's best-known arenas, was originally a converted railroad structure. It was covered in 1879 and could hold 11,000 spectators, but it was demolished ten years later to be replaced by a $3-million auditorium. However, in 1925 a new Madison Square Garden opened nearby, which was able to hold more than 18,000 people. It quickly became a popular place for sports events, and in 1946 more than five million people attended sports events there.

Left Wembley Stadium, built in 1923 in London, England, is being overhauled to include a huge sports and leisure complex.

The present Madison Square Garden opened in 1968, with a 20,000-seat arena, 48-lane bowling alley, exhibition hall, 5,000-seat forum and 11 escalators, together with its own police force and TV station. The evolution of "The Garden" is a good example of how sports arenas have developed over the years to accommodate an increasing number of events and a larger number of spectators.

More recent arenas are futuristic in their design. When the Huston Astrodome opened in Houston, in 1965, it was described as the

"ninth wonder of the world." Its steel dome and $24-million price tag made it the focus of much media attention, and it became home to the Houston Oilers football team, the Astros baseball team and many different sports events. The first artificial turf was installed here in 1965.

Right The Toronto SkyDome is the world's first major stadium with a fully retractable roof. It is constructed from three steel arches with a skin of PVC plastic on a steel deck. The illustration shows how the roof retracts in just twenty minutes. SkyDome is enormous — the roof spans 673 ft (205 m) at its widest point and is thirty-one stories high.

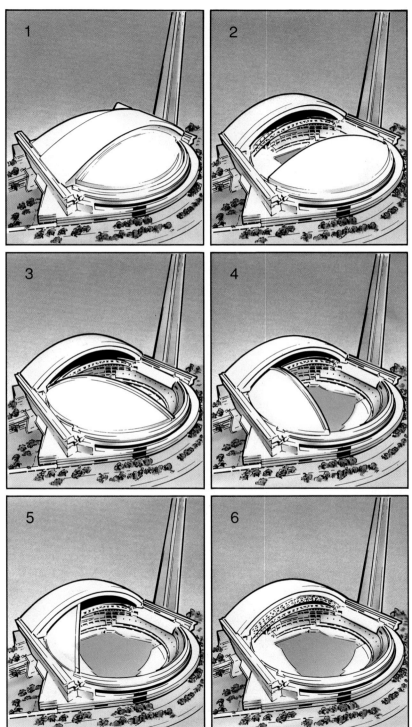

Opposite The multimillion-dollar New Orleans Superdome, where Superbowl XX is played.

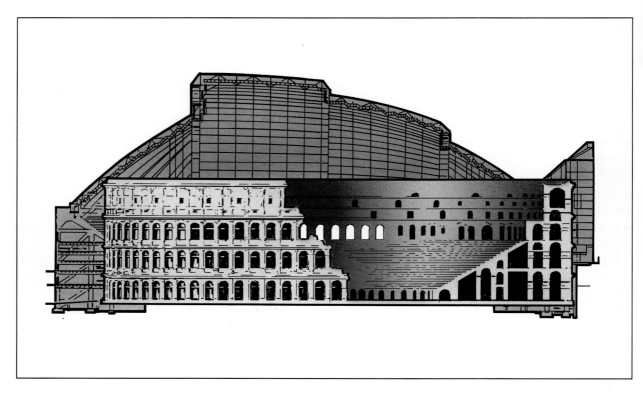

Ancient and modern – Rome's Colosseum (completed in AD 80) would fit easily inside the Toronto SkyDome.

Artificial turf seemed a great invention because it is so easily cared for. But it is a very hard surface and has been blamed for many injuries. Now the Huston Astrodome has been outshone by stadiums such as the New Orleans Superdome, which opened in 1975, costing over $100 million and seating 97,000 people under its own steel dome.

One of the most noteworthy stadiums is South Korea's Olympic Stadium and sports complex in Seoul. It was built especially for the 1988 Olympic Games. A fourteen-lane highway leads to the Stadium, and it has its own subway stop as well. There are separate facilities for baseball, track-and-field, water polo, basketball, swimming, gymnastics, weightlifting, cycling and fencing.

A technical marvel is Canada's Toronto SkyDome. The computer-designed, thirty-one stories high SkyDome was opened in 1989, at a cost of more than $500 million, and it was immediately heralded as the most innovative stadium ever built. Its huge roof can be opened or closed in just twenty minutes, so events can take place regardless of the weather. Its leisure facilities are of the highest standards and it is billed as "the world's greatest entertainment center."

The SkyDome is expected to revolutionize the design of stadiums, and its attractions include a 350-room hotel with 70 suites overlooking the field. It boasts restaurants, bars, health and fitness facilities, such as a pool and squash courts, a TV studio, the world's biggest video scoreboard, 115 ft × 33 ft (35 m × 10 m), and 161 private boxes. The seating is movable and is so arranged that up to 65,000 spectators can have an unobstructed view of sports events.

The SkyDome has set the standard for stadium design and it is no coincidence that when it was opened, the publicity included a note that Rome's ancient Colosseum could fit neatly inside it!

Equipment

In the competitive environment of today's professional sports, millions of dollars are spent trying to help players find "the edge" – that small improvement that means the difference between winning or losing. The technological development of sports equipment is helping them to reach for even higher goals.

Up to the 1980s, the world's great tennis players used wooden rackets. But wooden rackets were not strong enough for the new generation of powerful hitters, such as Jimmy Connors, Ivan Lendl and Boris Becker – something new had to be found.

At first, attempts were made to strengthen wood, often with plastic, but this made the rackets too heavy. Scientists then came up with what became known as graphite rackets, which are made of carbon fiber. These are specially reinforced with a material called Kevlar, which is more commonly used in the manufacture of bullet-proof vests and ceramic fibers. Today's rackets weigh less than a pound (340 g), with the heaviest component being the glue that holds all the parts together!

British technology has also come up with an injection-molded racket for which nylon and graphite granules are injected into a mold,

Old-style rackets could not have coped with Boris Becker's power.

Using a body bag, a hang-glider pilot can fly for hours without getting cold.

Below The parts of a hang-glider. Hang-gliders come in various shapes and sizes – some even look like conventional aircraft.

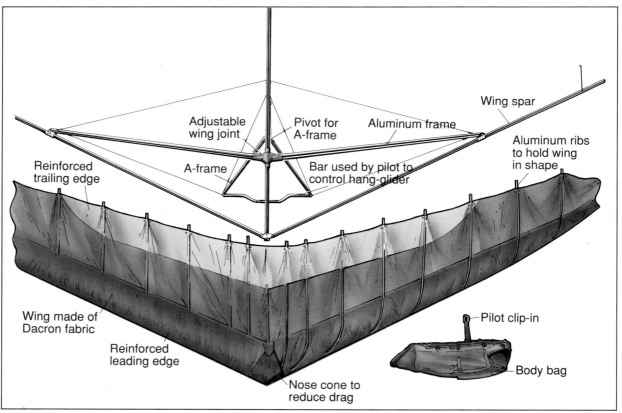

Wing spar

Adjustable wing joint

Pivot for A-frame

Aluminum frame

Aluminum ribs to hold wing in shape

Reinforced trailing edge

A-frame

Bar used by pilot to control hang-glider

Reinforced leading edge

Wing made of Dacron fabric

Pilot clip-in

Body bag

Nose cone to reduce drag

In the physically demanding sport of football, the players need the best protection.

which then sets like a cake. The key is lightness and strength, and so far technology has been able to find the solutions to the problems posed by men's tennis.

A similar problem was encountered in professional golf, with the advent of more skilled players and harder hitters. Old-style golf clubs were made from one piece of wood, usually hickory, and, since the 1930s, steel-shafted clubs have been popular. Graphite clubs are a recent development. Mostly cast from standard molds, the shafts are specially made and balanced for individual clubs. Even the "woods" are now made of plastic-coated metal.

Golf balls have also developed greatly. The original "feathery" ball was a leather bag crammed with goose feathers that had been soaked in water. This was sewn up, and when it dried it became rock hard. In 1899, Dr. Coburn Haskell from Cleveland, Ohio, invented a ball that had a hard rubber shell packed with elastic. The Haskell ball survived into the 1960s. But the players began to ask for a ball that gave them more control, particularly for spin. Several have been developed and the newest is the Bolata ball consisting of a rubber coating around a core of water or paste. The ball allows players to play shots with more dexterity, although the amateur finds it more difficult to hit for distance.

Some major developments have come in the physically demanding sport of football, where the players today need eighteen pieces of protective gear. Until the 1940s, players wore flimsy leather helmets or no helmet at all. As a result, there were a number of deaths. An American firm, the John T. Riddell Company, which manufactured pilots' helmets, then developed a plastic football helmet, which was adopted by the National Football League in the 1940s. All players were required to wear these helmets. Within ten years the "teardrop"

helmet evolved – the type of helmet that is still used today. The face guard, or "cage," came into general use in the 1950s. Most of today's players wear helmets with air-filled pockets, which are inflated when a player has the helmet on his head to ensure that it fits snugly and to provide cushioning.

As the game became more competitive in the 1960s, due in part to television coverage of games and increasing sponsorship, the players began to ask for all kinds of extra protection. Mouthguards, nylon shoulder pads, rib, arm and leg protectors and neck rolls, plus yards of protective tape around joints came into common use. In 1978, the inflatable rib protector was invented.

Mountain biking is one of the fastest-growing sports. It combines the speed of cycling on the road with the freedom to travel across the roughest country.

Bicycling has always been a popular sport. In the mid-1970s, BMX bikes were the rage. BMX stands for bicycle motocross, and the bicycles were built fot stunt riding over an obstacle course. Mountain bikes then started to become popular in the early 1980s, and today,

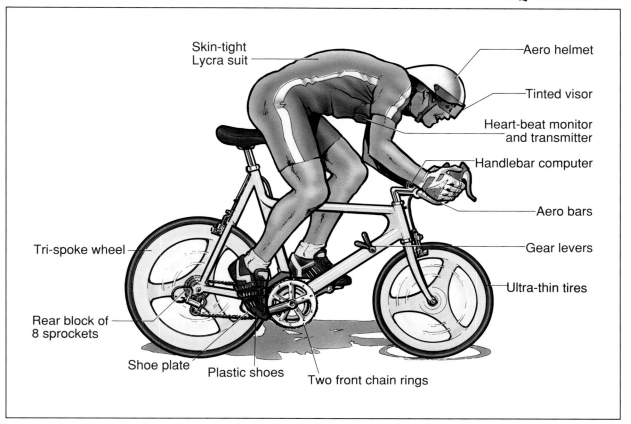

Skin-tight Lycra suit

Aero helmet

Tinted visor

Heart-beat monitor and transmitter

Handlebar computer

Aero bars

Gear levers

Ultra-thin tires

Tri-spoke wheel

Rear block of 8 sprockets

Shoe plate

Plastic shoes

Two front chain rings

The parts of a modern aerodynamic racing bicycle. The frames of some bicycles are made of a lightweight material called carbon fiber.

about 45 percent of all bikes sold are mountain bikes.

Mountain bikes are designed to travel over very difficult terrain. The pioneers, Gary Fisher and Charlie Kelly, from Marin County, California, made their bikes from whatever parts they could find on the garage floor. Heavy-duty parts are the feature of these bikes. Large, wide tires absorb the shock of rough ground; heavy wheel rims give strength and prevent wheel-buckling; 18-speed derailleur gears are essential for traveling up and down steep slopes; and the strong frame has to have the necessary clearances for the wide tires.

Mountain bikes are very different compared with the lightweight bicycles used by track and time-trial cyclists. In one design, the bicycle frame is made of carbon fiber and the tri-spoke wheels of molded Kevlar – disk wheels are sometimes used, but these are a disadvantage in windy conditions. "Aero bars" give the rider an aerodynamic position on the bicycle.

The rider will wear a Lycra suit and a streamlined helmet, and will shave his or her legs to reduce wind resistance. The shoes are made of plastic with rigid carbon soles and built-in shoeplates. These plates have slots that fit into the backplate of the pedal and fasten in place with clamps very similar to ski-boot bindings. A handlebar computer gives the distance the cyclist has traveled and the rider's speed. A heart-beat monitor will record the cyclist's pulse rate, which will later be analyzed for training purposes.

Comfort and ease of movement are essential elements of any type of sports clothing. The tracksuit in athletics became popular in the early 1920s, and little changed in terms of athletes' shirts and shorts until the 1980s, when figure-hugging bodysuits, made from a synthetic, elastic fabric called Lycra, appeared. The Lycra suits cut wind resistance and help to keep leg muscles and tendons warm, thus reducing the risk of injury while the athlete is performing. Lycra bodysuits are now used by many different sportsmen and sportswomen. Racing cyclists, swimmers and downhill skiers use the suits to help improve their performances.

Protection from the elements is also important. Golfers and mountaineers, for example, need to keep dry and comfortable when it is windy or raining. Up to the late 1970s, waterproof and windproof fabrics were either cotton or nylon that had been coated with an impervious layer of either wax or rubber.

Modern-day Argentinian Gabriela Sabatini, in nineteenth-century tennis clothes. Sports clothing design has come a long way in the last hundred years.

Above Speed skaters are among the many sports stars who rely on Lycra to cut wind resistance.

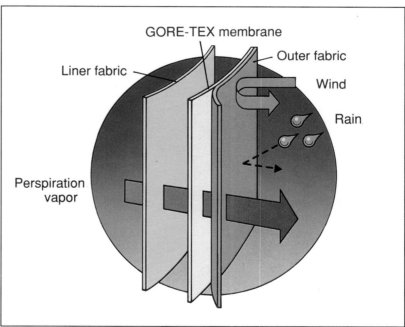

GORE-TEX membrane

Liner fabric

Outer fabric

Wind

Rain

Perspiration vapor

Right GORE-TEX, a fabric that "breathes," was invented in 1977.

The problem with these fabrics was that they did not allow perspiration from the body to escape, so the athlete might end up as "wet" inside the clothing as it was outside.

In 1977, a "breathable" fabric was invented by an American, Bob Gore. Called GORE-TEX fabric, it normally consists of three layers. Between the outer fabric and the lining is a membrane of PTFE – a material that has been engineered to contain 9 billion pores per square inch. Each pore is 20,000 times smaller than a droplet of water, forming an impenetrable barrier to wind, rain and snow. Yet each pore is 700 times larger

than a vapor molecule, allowing pespiration to escape from the body.

Breathable and waterproof fabrics are made into jackets, trousers, gloves, hats, socks, backpacks, tents and sleeping bags for a variety of sports activities, including track-and-field, skiing, golf, climbing, canoeing and cycling.

The wetsuit is worn by men and women who practice their sport on or under water. Made from neoprene – a rubber-based material – they come in many shapes and sizes, including a one-piece suit with short arms and legs (a "shorty"), a suit with long arms and legs (a "full" wetsuit) and a combination of the two.

Wetsuits are worn to keep the body warm – when people get so cold that their body temperature drops below normal, a very serious condition known as hypothermia results, which can be fatal if prolonged. Neoprene itself is waterproof, but most kinds of stitching are not. The more waterproof a wetsuit is, the warmer the person will be. In some wetsuits the panels are glued and "blind-stitched" – the neoprene is stitched through on one side only and has a "bead" of rubber sealant to glue the seams together. The thickness of the suit is important, too. The thicker the neoprene the warmer the wet suit will be. Often wetsuits are lined with Lycra to give a colorful and hard-wearing outer skin.

However, perhaps the greatest leap forward in sportswear technology has been in footwear. In the early days, there were shoes designed for specific sports, such as soccer, baseball, track-and-field and so on.

The uppers were all made of leather, with weighty leather or rubber soles, and the shoes were all very heavy and cumbersome.

One of the leading shoe companies in the world is Adidas, which, under the guidance of founder Adi Dassler, began making sports shoes in the 1920s. Dassler's main tasks were to reduce their weight and improve both durability and protection for the foot against injury.

By 1937 Dassler's range of shoes included thirty different models, and after World War II he founded the Adidas company and pioneered the soccer shoe with a molded sole for icy grounds, and then the revolutionary screw-in studs. Adi Dassler then went on to develop replaceable spikes and shock absorption in track shoes, both of which were used in the 1952 Olympics.

Throughout the 1950s and 1960s, new, lightweight materials, such as nylon, were used in the manufacture of sports shoes, and today more than fifty stages are used in the design process of a new shoe. These stages include key areas such as research, design, making a sample, durability testing, costing and bulk production, followed by delivery throughout the world.

Sports shoes are big business, and a major part of the budgets of shoe manufacturers is spent in advertising, encouraging athletes to wear their products, particularly at major sports events such as soccer's World Cup and the Olympics. From the steel toe-capped, water-sodden, heavy boots of the past, technology has created the super-lightweight, highly protective, adaptable and fashionable shoes of today.

Opposite Breathable fabrics, form an impenetrable barrier to rain and snow, yet allow perspiration to escape from the body, preventing clamminess. For many outdoor sports, clothing made from breathable fabric is now seen as essential.

Right Wetsuits are designed to protect divers from the cold.

The development of the wetsuit in the 1950s and 1960s enabled the spread of the exciting sport of surfing from warm seas to cold seas. The Polynesian islanders of the central Pacific were probably the first to ride waves – the famous explorer Captin Cook wrote about

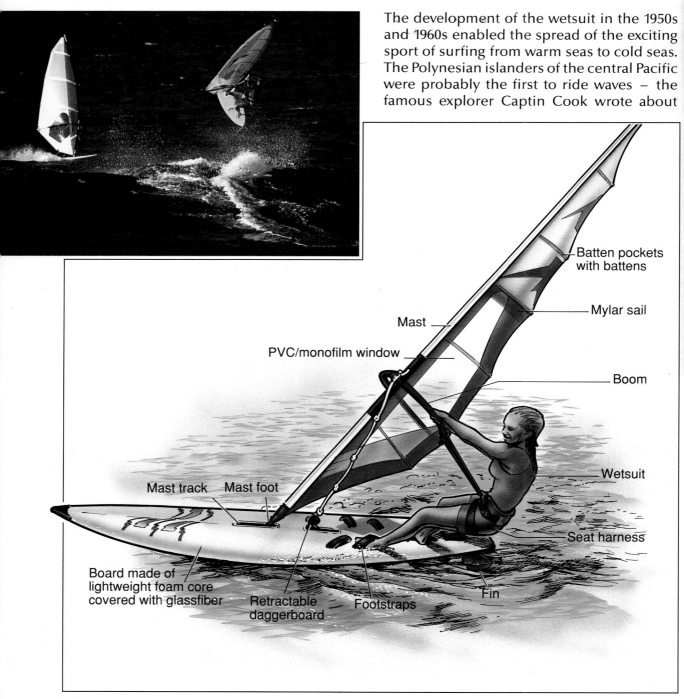

Batten pockets
with battens

Mylar sail

Mast

PVC/monofilm window

Boom

Wetsuit

Mast track   Mast foot

Seat harness

Board made of
lightweight foam core
covered with glassfiber

Retractable
daggerboard

Footstraps

Fin

Above The top women's surfer, Wendy Botha, during a surfing contest. Surfboards are made of lightweight plastic materials that make them maneuverable.

Opposite A windsurfing board. Shortboards do not have daggerboards. They are highly maneuverable and can be used for jumping off waves (inset).

the skill of the Hawaiians in 1778. In those days, surfboards were made of solid wood, and they were extremely heavy and difficult to maneuver. The innovations in plastics since World War II have revolutionized the sport. Plastic materials are also used in the making of windsurfing boards, the idea of which was first dreamed up in the late 1950s.

Surfboards and windsurfing boards have a lightweight foam core covered with glass-fiber or a similar material. Windsurfing boards are often reinforced with materials such as carbon fiber or Kevlar, to produce boards that are light, stiff and reasonably durable.

There are two basic types of windsurfing boards: longboards with a daggerboard (a big, removable fin in the middle, which stops the board from going sideways when sailing upwind), and shortboards, which are too short to build daggerboards into their hulls. Longboards are ideal for beginners. Special longboards are used for racing. Shortboards are very maneuverable and require a higher level of expertise to ride them.

Skiing is a perpetual quest for speed — every year ski manufacturers seem to come up with a new technological innovation that will improve the performance of ski equipment.

Most masts are made of glassfiber, although those for racing are more often made of aluminum, which is lighter and stiffer. Many sails are made of a synthetic material called Mylar, which is light, durable and waterproof. Windows in the sail help the windsurfer to see where he or she is going and to avoid hazards, such as other windsurfers. PVC/monofilm – a type of plastic – is often used for the window.

Every year, ski manufacturers seem to find new ways to make ski equipment perform just a little better. Plastic and synthetic materials have made skis lighter and easier to maneuver. One latest design has a fiberglass core protected with a plastic elastomer – a material that is able to bend without breaking. To help in turning and stopping, skis have steel edges that can be dug into the snow.

Slalom skis are narrower than other types of skis and are best for making quick turns. Some come with bent tips, which help to deflect the gate poles as the skier threads his or her way down the course.

Ski boots have changed dramatically since the 1960s, when people skied in boots that were really modified hiking boots. These boots were not altogether comfortable or easy to put on and take off. Modern ski boots are basically a plastic shell that can be put on either from the back or front. Front-entry types fasten by means of a padded tongue tightened by buckles. They are very popular with racers. Rear-entry boots are fastened with a hinged flap and use various methods to keep the heel down inside the boot.

Good binding design has almost halved skiing injuries over the last fifteen years. The bindings are spring-loaded clamps that are attached to the skis and hold down the ski boots. If the skier falls heavily, the binding springs open to release the boot from the ski.

Snowboarding is the newest snow sport. Instead of wearing two skis, the snowboarder uses a single, wide board about 55 to 65 in (140 to 165 cm) in length (skis are about 70 to 75 in (180 to 190 cm) in length). Racing boards are longer and stiffer than freestyle boards

Technology is already helping the new sport of snowboarding.

designed for doing jumps and tricks. "Soft boots" give freedom of movement and comfort and are used with freestyle boards. "Hard boots" give support and are used with racing boards. The boots and bindings are similar to their conventional skiing counterparts, except that the bindings do not have a quick release feature.

A few weeks before the opening of the 1988 Olympics, a 200-strong team of men and women, together with hundreds of tons of equipment, arrived in the South Korean capital of Seoul to begin their preparations for the Games. The numbers are not surprising, given that almost every nation sent a team to take part in the world's greatest sporting event. But this team of people was simply there to time those who were competing and not to compete themselves. The group comprised official timekeepers, scientists, computer wizards and technical magicians from the giant Swiss company, Omega.

The planning and organization involved in timing the Olympics is a far cry from the days when officials used stopwatches and clipboards to do their timing. Electronic timing has been used intermittently since the 1930s, but it was not officially adopted by athletics authorities until 1977.

In Seoul, computers were used to create what was, in fact, a "fourth dimension" in time and picture. The starting gun was wired to the starting blocks, which were fitted with sensitive pads, so that a computer could detect which athlete had made a false start. In addition, the gun triggered three cameras, two on the outside and one on the inside of the track, which took continuous exposure of the 100-m race, to produce a "time picture." The moment the race finished, judges and timekeepers had the finishing times displayed on television screens and the electronic scoreboard, but close scrutiny of the time picture enabled them to check the times for each athlete to a thousandth of a second.

All time-based sports make use of electronic

The starter's gun and sprinters' starting blocks are wired to a timing computer, which acts as a false start control system and gives timing of incredible accuracy.

technology to achieve timing of great accuracy. In Formula One auto racing, the timekeepers set up mini television stations around each Grand Prix circuit. Transmitters are carried in each car and relay information to specially-located timing points on the circuit. These measure the speed of the car and assess lap times, down to a thousandth of a second, which are then relayed to television screens in the pits, to the media and crowd.

At the Calgary Winter Olympics in 1988, a system was devised to measure the bobsled event, and no less than eighty special sensors were set up along the course. These were linked to a computer that could calculate the speed of each bobsled at any stage of the course, so that afterward the crews could

A time picture — the exact moment a race is won captured on film.

analyze on which part of the course they could improve their performance. Swimming pools are now built to accommodate pressure-sensitive timing pads, which are attached to each end of the pool. The pads are ⅜ in (1 cm) thick, so an extra ¾ in (2 cm) is added to the length of the pool. The pads are wired to a computer that gives incredibly accurate times for each swimming lane.

Timing is very important when a split-second can mean the difference between winning and losing. Once again technology has responded well to the changing and growing demands of sports.

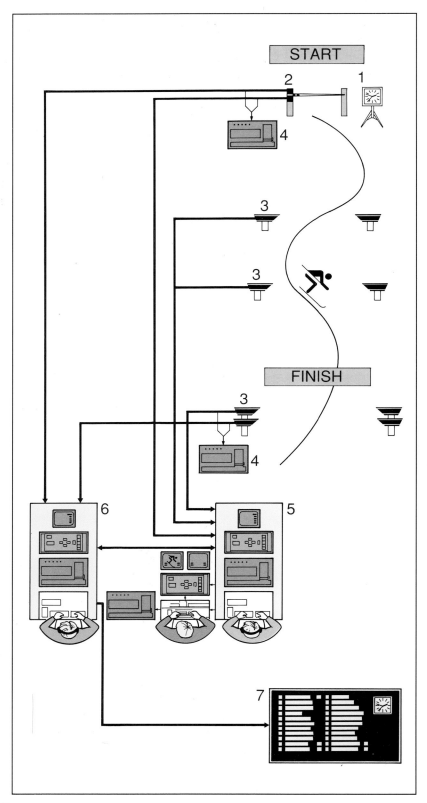

Modern timing systems can calculate the actual time of a competitor to one ten-thousandth of a second and automatically give his or her ranking during an event. The illustration shows the system used at a skiing event.

1. The synchronized start clock indicates the start to the competitor both visually and with sound.
2. When the skier goes through the start gate, it gives two simultaneous electrical impulses.
3. Photoelectric cells record the skier's time at various stages of a downhill course and a final time.
4. Two synchronized electronic counters are used in case of breakdown of the lines.
5. The principal timing control unit distributes timing information to the scoreboard, TV control room and to the race officials.
6. Backup timing control unit in case of a breakdown to the main timing control unit.
7. Scoreboard.

It has always been a challenge to find ways of improving an athlete's performance. At the Seoul Olympics, Canada's Ben Johnson won the 100 m in 9.79 seconds – with a peak speed of about 27 mph (43.5 kph). But when it was discovered that he had been taking performance-enhancing drugs, he was disqualified and stripped of his gold medal. America's second placed Carl Lewis became the champion in a time of 9.92 seconds, with a peak speed of 26.4 mph (42.5 kph).

The start of the 100 m at the 1936 Berlin Olympics. Note the cinder track.

Above High-tech starting blocks have helped runners to take off faster.

At the first Olympics, the winning time was exactly 12 seconds by America's Thomas Burke, but since then much has happened to enable athletes to run faster. That first Olympic final was held on a cinder track, with the athletes either standing or crouching with their feet in shallow holes they had dug to give them a firm start. Today, starting blocks have replaced the holes. Patented in the 1920s, the blocks did not come into widespread use until after World War II and were not used at the Olympics until the London Games in 1948. Modern blocks are adjustable and are made of aluminum or zinc-plated steel, with rubber-faced footplates set at an angle to reduce the stress on the athlete's legs as he or she "springs" into the race.

Tracks have also helped athletes to improve their times, and today's springier synthetic surfaces are ideal for the sprinter. They were

Left America's Florence Griffith-Joyner's 100-m world record time of 10.54 seconds in 1988 exceeded all expectations.

Opposite Today's swimwear is made to help swimmers move fast through the water.

of the new, skin-tight Lycra suits, which cut down wind resistance.

In 1980, a science convention in Manchester, England, devised a complex equation in order to predict at what time in the future, and by how much, athletics records would be set. The equation took into account such things as the energy of the runner, air resistance, altitude and running tracks. At the time, the scientists predicted that the world record for the men's 100 m in the year 2000 would be 9.82 seconds (a figure already surpassed by Johnson), and for the women's 100 m a time of 10.77 seconds (already surpassed by Florence Griffith-Joyner's 10.54 seconds in 1988).

Scientists have discovered that women's times in a variety of sports have improved at a faster rate than men's times. Today, women skate as fast as men did in 1960, and swim as fast as men in 1968. One reason for this trend is that women did not have the benefit of competing at an international level until relatively recently. In women's athletics, many race distances were not added to the Olympic program until the 1980s.

Speeds have improved in other events, such as cycling, skiing and rowing. Much of this improvement is put down to improved training and better equipment.

Swimmers' times have improved dramatically too. The men's 100-m freestyle was won in 1 minute 22.2 seconds at the first Olympics, in 1896. In Seoul, America's giant Matt Biondi won in 48.63 seconds. Studies in hydrodynamics, a branch of science concerned with the properties of liquids, have attempted to eliminate the drag of water on the body and helped improve the efficiency of swimmers, enabling them to go faster.

Modern swimwear – made from Lycra – is designed to reduce drag. Swimmers also shave their bodies before competition to make them more streamlined, and they wear goggles to enable them to see more clearly and so anticipate turns better. Antiwave ropes, which separate the lanes, cut down wash from neighboring swimmers in competition.

first used at the 1968 Mexico Olympics, replacing the old-style cinder tracks. In addition, athletes also have better coaching and training regimens, and they have the advantage

Training methods

Above Los Angeles Raiders linemen study defensive strategy at their training headquarters.

Opposite British runner Matthew Yates undergoes some scientific race preparations.

It is no coincidence that as science has become more closely involved in sports in recent years, training techniques have improved radically. Everyone is much more health and fitness conscious these days, and many people are prepared to work much harder on their personal fitness, diet and mental approach.

At the turn of the century, this combination would have been looked upon as complete lunacy. In athletics, training was limited to running and massage, and many athletes

relied on their innate ability rather than good coaching methods. There were professional coaches, but only athletes who were wealthy could benefit from an expert's tuition. Today, many nations can boast a vast network of coaching expertise for a wide variety of sports.

In some professional sports, there are a variety of coaches for a single team, each specializing in a particular area. For example, in the National Football League, teams boast an array of coaches for the offense, defense, quarterback, special plays and receivers. The teams also have an army of scouts to search for new talent in the high schools and colleges.

The United States has led the way in sports psychology, where mental toughness is as much a part of the athlete's armor as physical training and ability. Cus D'Amato, a legendary boxing manager, always stressed that fights were won and lost in the head. He ought to know. He managed two of America's world champions, Floyd Patterson and Mike Tyson. Based on skill and physical preparation, Mike Tyson should never have lost his undisputed world title to James "Buster" Douglas, in

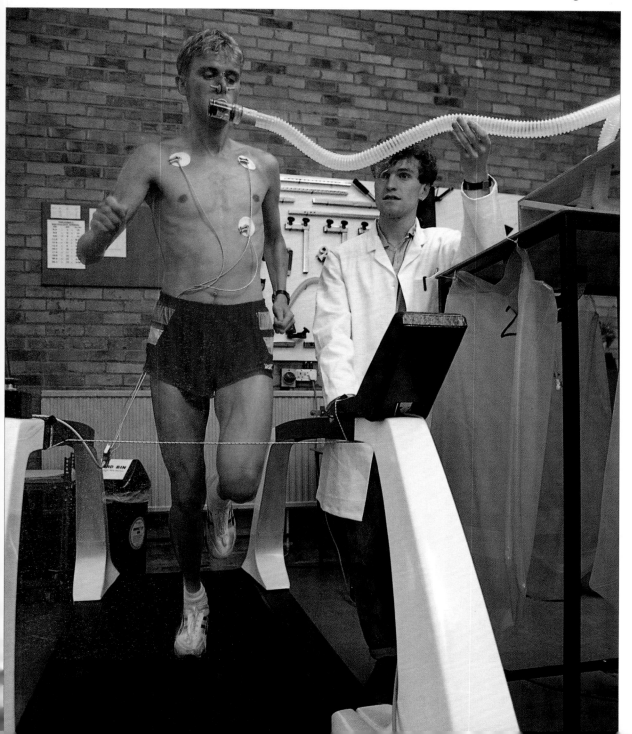

Tokyo, in 1990. He now admits he was not prepared mentally, and therefore his performance suffered.

Sports psychologists began by looking at the excuses athletes used for bad performances, such as loss of concentration, lack of aggression, or phrases such as "I talked myself out of it," or "I just wasn't feeling right today." The key to a winning mind is to root out self-doubt and improve concentration through visualization – actually running through in your mind what you want to do and how you want to play. Jack Nicklaus, an American who is arguably the world's greatest golfer ever, never played a shot in his life without first running it through in his mind. He described it as "going to the movies in my head."

Some top athletes have their own psychologists to sharpen their minds before major events. Now there are no excuses, and every top athletic performance is analyzed both physically and mentally.

Another facet of sports preparation that has improved dramatically is nutrition – a proper sports diet. It is not a new idea that the right food and drink aids performance, but technological advances in nutritional science and its application to the needs of different sports has meant it can make a discernible difference. Before the 1920 Olympics 100-m sprint final,

Right Computer technology is playing an increasing role in athletes' training programs. Here, a computer is used to measure performance during weight training.

Opposite Jack Nicklaus is a great exponent of "visualization" – a method of improving concentration by forming a mental image of what you want to do.

the four U.S. sprinters each drank a glass of sherry and a raw egg – a crude stimulant aimed at giving them a bit of extra pep before the race. It obviously paid dividends because they finished first, second, fourth and sixth.

Today, sports nutritionists can design energy-giving menus for different athletes, depending on their sport and how they train for it. They insist that the right food, allied to an intake of food supplements (extra vitamins and minerals), can develop the right body for a particular sport.

The nutritionists calculate the number of calories used by different athletes when they take part in their sport and draw up a complementary menu comprising fresh foods. For example, a lunch of 3.5 oz (100 g) of cheese, a mixed salad, a baked potato, a glass of orange juice, a banana and a cup of coffee, comes to enough calories to power a sprinter flat out for eighteen minutes or an archer for more than thirteen hours. Nutritionists look for a menu of around 3,000 to 4,000 calories each day, plus the vitamins, minerals and supplements the athlete needs.

31

In terms of pure technology, few sports have moved forward as fast as motorsports. Motorsports have been used as the testing ground for new designs of engines, bodies and chassis of racing cars, motorcycles and speed boats. If proved successful, the innovations are incorporated in production models.

The first official motor competition took place in 1894, on a dusty road between Paris and Rouen in France, where the winner completed the 79-mile (127-km) course with an average speed of 11.6 mph (18.6 kph). Interest in racing then rocketed, and Britain's first race track, called Brooklands, was built in 1906. The first Grand Prix was staged at Le Mans in France in the same year, and organizers had to impose a weight limit of 2,182 lb (992 kg) because the cars were getting so big. The engine sizes also grew larger, and during the 1920s limits were imposed on their size.

Left The performance of a car is affected by its shape — air resistance is kept to a minimum by making the car low and with a smooth, curving shape. The wings seen on Grand Prix cars and some sports cars produce a downforce that improves road holding at high speeds.

The angular shape of the family car causes turbulance over the rear of the car.

The racing car's aerodynamic shape allows air to flow over it without causing turbulance.

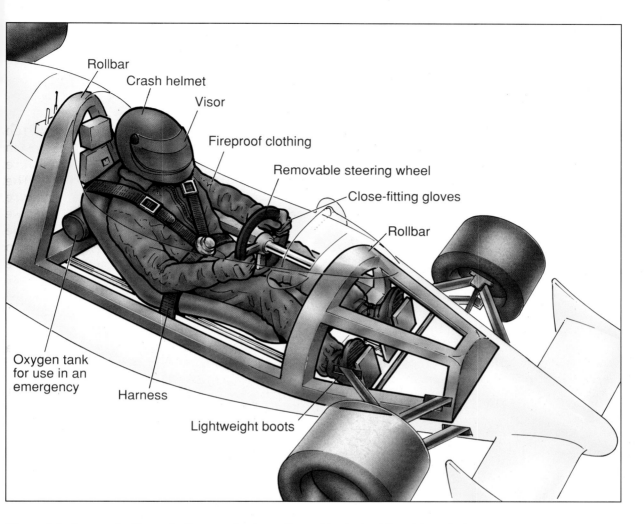

Rollbar

Crash helmet

Visor

Fireproof clothing

Removable steering wheel

Close-fitting gloves

Rollbar

Oxygen tank
for use in an
emergency

Harness

Lightweight boots

The safety frame of a Formula One car is strengthened to protect the driver during a crash. Grand Prix safety improvements mean crashes are now rarely fatal.

The 1930s saw the development of the super-charger, a device that meant that small capacity engines could be literally "blown" into much more powerful machines. It does this by increasing the amount of air taken into the engine to boost performance. This led to a split in the classification of racing cars, and after World War II unsupercharged engines could be as big as 2,999 cc whereas supercharged cars had to be 4,490 cc or less.

But it was in 1977 that the biggest impact on auto racing was first felt – the turbocharged Renault. Like superchargers, turbo power vastly increased the power output of an engine, only much more markedly. In turbocharged engines, a pump driven by the engine's exhaust increases the pressure on the gases inside the engine. The high pressure increases the force of the combustion inside the engine's cylinders. Turbocharged cars can go considerably faster than cars with the same size, non-turbocharged engines.

Safety standards in today's auto racing events are stringent, but there are still accidents, and the history of Grand Prix racing has seen many fatalities. The driver's cockpit is now strengthened by carbon fiber able to withstand horrific-looking crashes. On impact, major parts break away in such a way that drivers are not injured by flying debris. Every car has a sophisticated high-pressure fire extinguishing system, which can put out fires that often follow a crash.

Banked areas, which are designed to slow down cars on fast corners, and wide run-off areas are standard features of racing tracks around the world. On modern circuits marshaling is more effective and circuit organization much more coordinated, with officials, doctors and accident and first-aid equipment situated all around the track.

Powerboat racing is now becoming more popular. Some of today's powerboats are capable of speeds in excess of 137 mph (220 kph) and the acceleration from their .50 gal (2-liter) engines is a phenomenal 0–99 mph (0–160 kph) in just 4.2 seconds. Any powerboat, including a ski boat with a top speed of 40 mph (65 kph) can, given choppy conditions, become airbourne. However, in races, time spent in the air is time spent without the push of the engines, so it is avoided as much as possible.

Technology has done much to increase the speed and power of the motorcycle, too. The first motorcycle races were recorded at the end of the nineteenth century in Britain, but because of a speed limit of 20 mph (32 kph) they were forced to look for "off-road" circuits and "offshore" races, such as the Isle of Man, where the famed TT (Tourist Trophy) Races have been staged since 1907.

The first motorcycles were crude, single-cylinder machines, with 2-in (5-cm) diameter tires and mudguards and pedals to help the riders up steep hills. In 1920, a four-stroke Sunbeam motorcycle completed the 226.5-mile (364.5-km) race at an average speed of 51.8 mph (83.38 kph). In 1984, a 750 cc Honda completed the course at an average speed of 118.28 mph (190.35 kph). The motorcycle was built to high-tech racing specifications including a two-part radiator system for maximum cooling power, electronic fuel injection and a lightweight metal alloy frame.

Millions are spent on perfecting motorcycles for the racing circuit.

Racing boat designs

Racing boats have two basic hull designs – displacement and planing. Motorboats with displacement hulls ride in the water. Those with planing hulls skim over the water's surface. Hydroplanes are the most common planing boats. The bottom of the hull is flat or slightly curved. A flat-bottom boat has gently sloped sides. The boat may have engines either inside or outside the hull. A tunnel hull has long "floats" that extend the length of each side, creating a "tunnel" down the middle. A V-bottom hull has steeply slanted sides with a pointed bottom. These hulls perform well in rough water.

Hydroplane

V-bottom hull

Flatbottom hull

Tunnel hull

Positive drug tests marred the 1988 Olympic weightlifting competition.

Technology has not been a completely beneficial force on the world of sports. As sports have become more competitive, prize money and prestige have grown, and thus the incentive to win has vastly increased. Technology has played a key role in developing short cuts to success, in simple terms, cheating.

The use of performance-enhancing drugs has spread since the late 1960s, when the "power" athletes, notably bodybuilders, weightlifters, field event throwers and football players, began experimenting with them. Athletes turn to drugs in the belief that drugs will help them to run faster or longer, and help them to train better or build up muscles.

Drug taking has had a chilling "domino effect" in world sports, as athletes began to think that if they did not take drugs they would never win. As one notable drug taker admitted: "If you're not on anything it's like lining up on the blocks wearing trainers when everyone else is in spikes."

The following are some of the dangerous substances that have invaded the world of sports:
• **Stimulants** are aimed at giving athletes a short high, leaving them ultra wakeful.
• **Steroids** and hormones build up body muscle and encourage the development of body tissue.
• **Narcotic analgesics** are strong painkillers.
• **Betablockers** slow down the heart rate and encourage calmness.
• **Diuretics** reduce weight by removing water from the body.

Many performance-enhancing drugs are banned by official bodies such as the International Olympic Committee (IOC) and the International Amateur Athletics Federation (IAAF). The IAAF's current banned list extends to hundreds of drugs in many different categories. The positive testing of Canadian sprinter Ben Johnson came at a time when the authorities were starting to address the drugs problem. Not only was Johnson the greatest sprinter of all time and the reigning world champion, but he was caught in the full glare of the world's media after smashing the world record and winning the 100-m sprint at the 1988 Seoul Olympics.

Ben Johnson wins the 100 m at the 1988 Seoul Olympics. He was then tested positive for the banned steroid, Stanozolol, and stripped of his gold medal.

Humans are not the only racers at risk from drugs — race horses have been given drugs to improve their performances as well.

Johnson had been taking steroids for some years. He said they enabled him to train longer and harder, build up muscle and come into competitions far more aggressively. In terms of carrying the anti-drug message, the Johnson episode did much to focus attention on improving drug detection and rooting out the cheaters.

Johnson served his punishment (a two-year ban) and returned to athletic competition. He plans to race at the Olympic Games in Barcelona in 1992. Some people think all drug takers should be banned from competitive

athletics for life, while others believe that they should be given a second chance once they have proved they are no longer taking performance-enhancing drugs.

The side effects of steroids, the most widely used drug in sports, can be very serious and in some cases have caused deaths. A twenty-six-year-old bodybuilder died recently from liver cancer after taking steroids for some years. Steroids can also contribute to the risk of heart disorders and cause sterility.

Stimulant overdoses have also caused sports deaths in recent decades: a Danish cyclist died during an Olympic race in 1960, and a world championship cyclist died during the Tour de France in 1967. In both cases the drug responsible was an amphetamine, which is used to intensify performance and helps athletes to shrug off sports injuries.

Blood doping is another method that is used to improve performance. An athlete has red blood cells removed from his or her blood, and when the body has replaced the cells itself, the removed cells are returned to the blood. With an increase in red blood cells, the athlete has an increased but temporary advantage because he or she is able to carry more oxygen in the blood, which aids performance in long-distance events.

Drug detection was first introduced at the Olympics, in Mexico, in 1968, although the first steroid tests were not conducted until 1976.

Urine samples are collected randomly – in training or competition – and tested for banned substances. A disciplinary procedure is put into action if even the smallest trace is found.

In 1986, IOC-accredited laboratories around the world discovered 687 cases of banned substances being used by athletes. The following year, the figure had risen to 924, while in 1988 it totaled 1,353 (which included the Olympics), and in 1989 (a quieter year for athletics) the figure was 1,341.

Despite the Johnson saga and the vast sums of money that have been spent on drug detection techniques, it seems that drug taking is still as big a menace as ever, and sports authorities around the world are now discussing what new means are available to stop what has become an extremely undesirable development.

A laboratory technician checks samples in test tubes. There are many drug-testing laboratories operating around the world.

Television has contributed greatly to the development and popularization of sports. Before global television coverage was possible, sports events were staged before a "live" crowd and relayed to millions of others in the early days by newspapers alone, and then from the 1920s by radio. Today, every major international sports event – and thousands of smaller ones – are beamed into our homes via satellite.

In London, in 1936, the BBC (British Broadcasting Company) began its first regular television service. *The Times* newspaper of London suggested that television would "give the opportunity to satisfy an eager public" and that "all the doings of the great world would take on new life and interest." The newspaper was right, and in the first years of television broadcasting, the management of the BBC looked upon sports as a good way to guarantee

Television cameras ready to capture the best soccer action. Instant slow-motion replay is a feature of sports coverage.

The standard of television coverage has improved thanks to the use of remote-controlled cameras that are positioned to give an unusual view of a sports event.

a mass audience. But it took time for TV technology to come to terms with sports coverage, first in recorded form, and then with live transmissions of major events.

In 1939, America's NBC television station transmitted its first outside broadcast – a baseball game between Princeton and Columbia Universities. In those days, the pictures were not very clear or sharp, and the best sports coverage was restricted to small arena events, such as boxing and tennis, rather than sports such as soccer and baseball. It was not until the 1948 Olympics that the BBC, still in the forefront, managed to improve its cameras enough to make coverage of field sports worthwhile. The Image Orthicon camera had three interchangeable lenses and a viewfinder that, unlike previous cameras, gave the image the right way up. This

made it easier for the cameramen to get the best pictures, and the standard of coverage improved.

In the 1950s and 1960s, most field events were covered by just four large cameras and with no action or slow-motion replays. These came at the end of the 1960s and could be used only after an event had been recorded and then edited to produce a report that showed the highlights. Instant replay was introduced in November 1961 by ABC Television Sports, and today, there is instant slow-motion replay for any part of a live game.

The medium on which sport is recorded has also changed. Sixteen millimeter film was replaced by 2-inch (51.8-mm) magnetic tape, which was physically cut during the editing process. Today, half-inch tape (12.7 mm) is the norm; it can be edited at the touch of a button. Digital tape, which records pictures as

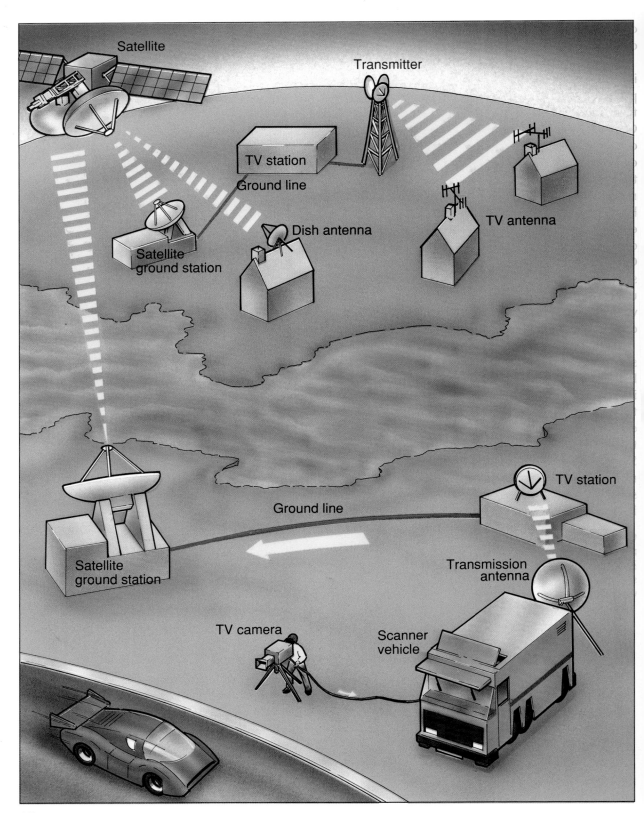

Satellite

Transmitter

TV station

Ground line

Satellite ground station

Dish antenna

TV antenna

TV station

Ground line

Satellite ground station

Transmission antenna

TV camera

Scanner vehicle

computerized digits, will greatly improve the quality and clarity of pictures.

A major landmark in television coverage is the use of satellite technology to relay pictures around the world. Satellites were first used to send pictures from the Olympic Games in Tokyo, in 1964. But the receiving country had little or no control over which events were received. Since then, satellite technology has improved beyond recognition, and the number of satellites has increased greatly, so that any sports event in any country can be transmitted to our television screens. At the 1988 Seoul Olympics in Korea, most major broadcasters secured in advance the use of satellites and used them to send pictures of the events that would be of interest to their viewers in their own countries.

The first color transmissions of sports started in the United States in 1953. In Britain, the BBC introduced color pictures in 1967, while in places like Australia, color television was not introduced until the early 1970s. By the mid-1970s, advances in technology in Britain, Europe and the United States had given sports television new meaning. Football, baseball, soccer, winter sports, indoor sports and the Olympics all looked so much more real.

Satellite television has also brought a new dimension to sports enthusiasts around the world, as there are channels that specialize in transmitting major sports events. Television companies now use mini cameras and advanced sound equipment to improve sports coverage. For example, football players have been wired for sound, and, in 1991, cameras were even attached to the helmets of some quarterbacks for an unforgettable head-on view of a charging linebacker.

Mini cameras are a relatively new idea, but over the last few years they have been gradually introduced into many different sports. They are about the size of a cigar and can be mounted almost anywhere – goalmouths, Formula One racing cars, hockey pucks and skateboards, for example.

New advances in television technology will add significantly to the enjoyment of sports fans. The wide screen and high-definition television with its cinemascope picture could mean the end of the ordinary sets and the introduction of screens, like mini movie theaters, in the home. Added to that will be stereo sound, with special sound effects. The aim of television sports coverage has always been to bring the event to the viewer – soon the viewer will feel as if he or she is actually at the event.

Opposite The satellite has revolutionized the television industry – now events can be seen live from anywhere in the world.

Right A mini camera in an ice hockey goal shoots some close-up action.

Glossary

Amphetamine One of several dangerous synthetic drugs that increase physical and mental activity, prevent sleep and decrease appetite. In athletics, the drug increases alertness and may quicken reflex action. Although they are stimulants, misuse of amphetamines can lead to exhaustion, depression and death.

Bobsled A racing sled for two or more people, with a steering mechanism enabling the driver to direct it down a steep, icy course.

Carbon fibers Fine, black silky threads, each thinner than a human hair. When used as a reinforcement they can make a material much tougher.

Cinder track An old-style running track made of the material that is left after the burning of coal or coke. Today's running tracks are made of artificial materials.

Coach A trainer or instructor who prepares athletes for competition.

Concourse A large open space in a stadium where people can gather before taking their seats.

Digital Concerned with information in the form of numbers or digits. Digital tape is a magnetic tape on which pictures and sounds can be recorded digitally, giving high-quality reproduction.

Four-stroke engine An internal combustion engine in which a piston makes four strokes for every explosion. In a four-stroke cycle, a piston moves down, sucking fuel into the cylinder (1). The piston rises again, compressing the mixture (2). A spark ignites it and the gases produced force the piston down (3). Finally, the piston rises pushing the burned gases out of the cylinder (4).

Fuel injection A system for introducing fuel directly into the combustion chambers of an internal combustion engine.

Gladiatorial combat A fight between trained warriors to entertain the ancient Romans. Most gladiators were prisoners of war, slaves or criminals. Often they were forced to fight to death in these contests.

Grand Prix This is a French term that means "large prize," and is any of a series of races in which Formula One cars compete.

Graphite A soft, black material that, in carbon fiber form, is used for tough, lightweight sports equipment.

Hydrodynamics Th ebranch of science concerned with the mechanical properties of fluids — the laws of hydrodynamics describe the behavior of flowing liquids. Scientists and designers apply these laws to the design of boats.

Injection molding A method of shaping an object by introducing a fluid under pressure into a mold.

Lycra A type of synthetic elastic fabric and fiber that is used for running suits and bathing suits.

Magnetic tape A long strip of plastic tape that has been impregnated or coated with crystals of iron oxide. The tape is used to record sound or video signals.

Minerals A class of inorganic substances, many of which are needed by the body in very small amounts, such as iodine, copper, manganese, iron and cobalt.

Nutritionist A person who has studied the role of food in bodily processes such as growth, energy production and repair of body tissues.

Psychologist A person who is engaged in the study of the mind and human behavior.

Satellite An artificial device orbiting around the earth — a communications satellite is used for receiving, amplifying and re-transmitting radio or television signals.

Starting block An adjustable device with pads against which a sprinter braces his or her feet in a crouch start.

Steroid One of a large group of compounds that is used illegally by some athletes to build up muscles and encourage the development of body tissue.

Synthetics Artificially created substances in which two or more elements are combined to make a compound. Plastics and fibers such as acrylic and nylon are synthetic materials.

Tournament A sports event in which contestants play a series of games to determine an overall winner.

Vitamin One of a group of chemical compounds that the human body needs in small amounts.

Further reading

Gardner, Robert. *Science and Sports.* (Franklin Watts, 1988)

Kettelkamp, Larry. *Modern Sports Science.* (William Morrow, 1986)

Mohun, Janet. *Drugs, Steroids and Sports.* (Franklin Watts, 1988)

Sports and Recreation (11 Volumes). (Raintree Publications, 1987)

Acknowledgments

The author would like to thank the following for their help in the writing of this book: Adidas (UK) Ltd, Amateur Rowing Association, Amateur Swimming Association, British Association for the Advancement of Science, Cantabrian, Dunlop-Slazenger, IAAF, Lonsdale, Motorsport Magazine, National Football League, Omega Electronics Ltd, Ontario House, Alan Pascoe Associates, Raleigh, Reebok, Speedo, Sports Council, Wimbledon Tennis Museum.

The publishers would like to thank the following for allowing their photographs to be reproduced in this book: Aldus Archive 25 (bottom); Bob Allen 12; Allsport 4 (bottom, Simon Bruty), 5 (Adrien Murrell), 6 (bottom, Mike Powell), 9 (Bob Martin), 10 (top, Didier Givois), 14, 15 (top, Mike Powell), 16 (Mike Powell), 17 (Kurt Amsler), 19 (Jean-Pierre Lenfant), 22 (left, Howard Boylan), 26 (Jean-Marc Barey), 28 (Mike Powell), 29 (Gray Mortimore), 30 (David Cannon), 34 (Pascal Rondeau), 37 (Mike Powell), 38 (Jun Nicholson), 41 (Ruusell Cheyne), 43 (Bob Martin); W L Gore & Associates 15 (bottom); Omega 23; Science Photo Library 39; Sporting Pictures 4; Topham 14 (left), 36; Ultra Sport (UK) Ltd 18, 20, 21; Wembley Stadium Ltd 6 (top); ZEFA *cover*, 11, 25 (top), 27, 31. Artwork by Brian Davey.

Index